Last Poems

Last Poems

Thomas Sanfilip

ARA PACIS

Copyright © 2007 by Thomas Sanfilip

All rights reserved. Except for brief passages quoted for reviews, this book may not be reproduced in whole or in part, in any form without permission from the author.

Manufactured in the United States

First edition

Grateful acknowledgement to the University of Chicago Press for permission to quote from the Richmond Lattimore translation of *Agamemnon* by Aeschylus from *The Oresteia, Aeschylus I, Compete Greek Tragedies*, University of Chicago Press© 1953.

Ara Pacis Publishers
P.O. Box 1202
Des Plaines, Illinois 60017-1202

Library of Congress Control Number: 2007902692

ISBN 13: 978-0-9625306-5-4

Last Poems

*Now as this bed stricken with night and drenched with dew
I keep, nor ever with kind dreams for company:
since fear in sleep's place stands forever at my head
against strong closure of my eyes, or any rest:
I mince such medicine against sleep failed: I sing,
only to weep again the pity of this house
no longer, as once, administered in the grand way.
Now let there be again redemption from distress,
the flare burning from the blackness in good augury.*

Aeschylus

I

1

What is it in that staggered memory
that drifts, blinding the furtive energy I struggle to arrest?
I'm measuring with one touch its white shadow,
but emptiness blankets the path, a harsh scrapping,
endless shoveling that reveals only where my steps begin.

2

No need to speak if the rain falls,
silence waking simplistic words…
if I speak words, I keep speaking words,
if I insist what's written need be written again.

3

Along the seam of my heart the flora & fauna of anxiety,
my mother's open throat, shadows across her face,
reproductions of misery & love,
my bleeding resignation, my heart's psychic drama,
my sister's denuded scapulas…
what more left to open my veins against this humid light
waiting to strike the final blow?

4

Father,
your cavernous walk
is that tacit molecule of time pinched in pain,
biting your head, waiting on death,
the dog sleeping, head inclined to hand,
rolling over old stock into dying efforts at your feet.
You wake the dog in steps to the door,
life hinging on that tail wag,
your only friend, you say, walking next to the light
circling the porch, dying among new blossoms,
blowing straight home in whirlwinds around you,
mother tending without protest plants she gathers,
giving up her heart, knowing the dissipation.

5

No one knows I've always been
walking quietly around the thirty per cent loss,
the key to other steps I never take when you look up with
terror in your eyes, proving the whole of existence is some
venous contortion of old age,
surprised the sun fades into manageable fragments
with a silence that surprises even me.

6

My hand swipes the air,
watching with sleepy eyes weeds come pouring out
the ground late afternoon,
stuck at an interlude of mindless peace,
interesting only for the door a few feet away,
the measured steps of mother in the yard.
How many more years your easy indifference?
I'm underneath measuring the foundation,
wondering why it's all over or beginning,
the whole absurd mess explained in a book,
generating a few worthless laughs, a few hits of ridicule,
as if our throats cut for an instant,
the sun a sliver on the lawn,
dog asleep, mother making one last trip backyard.

7

That table my sister sits at is square in its loneliness,
her pathetic bowl of soup so pointless,
it wallows wormlike at the end of her spoon.
I walk in by chance having no idea the table is so square,
so lenten in its religious stupidity,
making me cry her loneliness that isn't worth living,
her slow walk no one wanted, her pain no one desired,
her suffering that has no smile,
killing me with her ruptured heart.

8

I pour eternally into the venue a bleak light,
an old shadow lying in bed,
naked to the sheet,
roused from stupor at 1 a.m. stretched across the floor,
reaching the door before a soft whisper
scrapes along the street,
cutting perfect black sheets of rain,
stepping two steps astride this poor poetic impulse.

9

Sunday has its quiet fear hiding in my chest.
I anticipate their naked wound
when my attention is lapse,
each one sleeping a dream of tired adrenals,
that anyone cares enough to care,
that I've done right by tossing this dead branch
far from home, stretching our credibility to a god forsaken
truth I've even lost strength to witness.

10

Mother,
you're standing at the window
waiting for me to throw away the branch.
For what, I ask–confirmation, assurity, peace of mind?
I'm not sure the path is clear to the trees.
I'm telling you,
the branch you put in my hands doesn't speak its cause,
doesn't lament its fate,
more human than vegetal even to a patch of lawn.

11

I didn't expect your peaceful quietude,
you and father, two insoluble spirits joined wordless,
cooling your eyesight on the end
where like a dream I leave you both half-human,
half-statue, surprised you're not behind me
before the work is finished,
before the chiropractic exercise,
beyond these leaves that trap the voice
on pleasantries fall to the ground
because wherever a worthless cause,
we know the burdens that make us one.

12

I sleep below the edifice
that weighs us down to the debris,
telling you in resigned whispers
the same breath is always melancholy,
having no price we haven't paid,
holding in our words until
not even we have time left to taste the bread.

13

Father,
I hardly understand the bond that fuses your misery
into hyperbolic vulgarities,
facing your daughter whose only reason for living
perhaps is to teach us the misery of existence,
lashing you like animals,
raging back in some back-and-forth concerto of sheer
hatred, testing the brink, waiting for the trauma
that sends you & her to your knees,
having no recourse, but time,
slapping death across the face.

14

The sun is so beautiful today,
the stagnant air in this house so perpetual & stifling,
dead & lifeless.
Maybe they'll listen to the dictates of the vigil,
the ramifications of one death over another
to placate the struggle.

15

My depression
lives a strange undercurrent I can't identify,
strangling me just below the surface of my thoughts
where I can't reach existence,
somehow surviving the recurring metaphors of my birth.
Maybe each step is emptiness fulfilled,
training to realize one avenue of survival is one
to absolute purity.

16

Silence descends,
a dead loneliness twisted below the clavicle
inside the roots, shadows across each night,
a quiet hysteria that makes me calm as it worsens,
the great downward spiral of my birth resurrected
when the flower's living emptiness dominates.
This point is set against the world,
no longer a reach I have walking through self-pity
in strange poetic garb.

17

I want to find zen,
but my mind falls into emptiness,
the moon surrounded by a last blue bit of sky
that surprisingly appears in the worst emptiness
one can experience when, instead of enlightenment,
I find sleep.

18

Looking up from below,
I hear a drugged silence seventeen minutes after noon.
I'm thinking of my mother's involuntary tears, listening,
advising, suffering, suggesting,
carrying one final gesture of hope.
Sometimes I realize there's misery
no matter how proud some moment of grief,
biology having had its way,
resurrecting not one iota of happiness
without torture or regret.

19

That melon's clean, sliced, yellow flesh spilling wet seeds,
lolling on one side,
reminds me of a brutal asphyxiation,
the interior of my mind,
the residue of bright thoughts,
my father smiling for the cheapness of the coup.
These victories nourish the body,
but this melon is the soul,
the ripped-out territory of manhood,
the transfixed gaze he brings on unexpectedly,
not knowing whether to turn my eyes away,
or sheared clean through to the image of my heart,
shocking me speechless.

20

How does your daughter escape the fact she's dying,
chemicalized in twilight,
every time there's obstacles,
every time the needle slips in to drain & recycle
all the formaldehyde from her thoughts?

21

Yesterday
the bundle of branches they tied
with thin white string
hung limply from their fingers.
Almost pathetically they laced the stack
in the loosest, most delicate manner,
string swaying absurdly from fingertips,
looking down on that bundle of green,
pausing a moment to decide whether going this
way or that, this weak white string,
reminiscent of their endeavors,
an act so futile & pathetic, holding nothing
but the knot.

22

At sixty-nine
few moments of lucidity are yours.
Even you agree you're masochistic,
the protective device that helps you modify reality.
If I could only show you what it looks like inching on,
always at the edge of that last leap into oblivion,
that mad, tortured glare that comes with your death-wish,
your need for reprieve,
everything you say is irretrievable.

23

The street forces me to its peripheral limits,
endless like some tragic memory,
brightened by other memories
whispering in the dark,
forcing the issue,
my chest pressed painfully to the bedstead
twisted around my ribs.
I lie back with shallow breath,
painting the mask that covers my mood,
fumbling for words to explain my vigilance,
leaving me haunted with rhetoric,
a brief mercy & misery coming forth from emptiness,
recognizing the predator
that crawls from beneath my sleep.

24

I was surprised to see them together,
a radiation of light over their transfixed faces,
closer than I imagined,
listening, not to each other, but a disembodied voice,
sketching out the perimeter of their lives, never listening,
relentless, silent, withdrawn into a screen
that talks of nothing private or familiar,
but what they know well…
the fear of feeling the weakest portion,
the sub-structure of time,
confidants no closer to the truth of each other's lives,
overwhelmed & tired of sacrifices,
collapsing already into the dreary silence of the numb.

25

Like shattered poems,
their crude vulgarities persist.
Already they know the inevitable walking on knees that
hardly bend,
hating in the loving murder,
instinct supporting their mercurial dance,
poisoning the bright human spirit of reprieve
they won't yield,
suffering memories before they've finished their brutalities.

26

The stones are no longer useful,
cluttering the lower world,
strength destroyed,
imageless, denuded, not even earthlike,
taking but two hands to rearrange their order,
separating thought from feeling,
meaning from substance,
one existence from another, having no more shadow
under the sky.
My arms are long enough to reach them,
not knowing where they could be useful,
using my arms to dissuade their ascent into a blaze
of sun & wind today in separate piles,
their soft, grey roundness underwater after relentless rain,
resting secure like the last weight,
the sun moving in serene orbit above our heads,
as though hands wringing this dispossession
no longer theirs.

27

Father,
that gaze that looks at me so helplessly
revolves inside an orbit of miserable perplexity,
reduced to one eye that turns woe-begone a helpless gaze
for want of pity, love, perhaps again your moment
of glory as spoiled child.
Who knows if the fact is there that won't frighten you,
absolving the responsibility that will undo you as father,
everything reduced to one lonely, frightened hope,
fighting all the paradoxes one man can stand?

28

The grass bends in endless strength
bearing up the fears that have taken us to this–
the child's brief good-bye,
the hand with its violent morbidity
having felt nothing until now,
a soft breeze portending rain or worse,
only time to reject the fact having become religion,
having lost the view they cannot endure
with all resistance the purest flower of the mind.

II

1

Three forms make their way through dark:
mother, father, daughter,
tracing steps through overgrowth,
more Dantesque than Shakespearean,
murdered living forms engaging the dance of death.

2

The guitar rests calmly in your grip, father,
but you can hardly press its strings,
strength vanished from your fingers,
staring in weak surprise as you grip the neck,
wondering if it's in tune until I play,
singing that loose bond protecting us from the sky,
the sound too weak, too secret to admit
the final utterance I hear in your voice.

3

Apples
no bigger than marbles fall prematurely
to the ground one by one
like drops of water
singing in time to our plaintive voices
lost among the leaves.

4

There's no conspiracy but the suffering, sister,
that last horrible oracle of madness we've feared,
but silently borne with your walk,
backward down stairs,
realizing in two strokes,
with hardly a second to ourselves,
all the energies
of your slowing walk, sallow shade, tortured head
we sense time running out,
death waiting for the quick strike,
spouting memories at the kitchen table,
arm scarred with clotted blood,
a thousand punctures having recycled existence,
when there's no answer to be found,
no one to die in your place,
no one to openly bear–as you say–
the sickening smell of death.

5

Father,
we turn to see your weary, unsmiling droop of a body,
crushed by eighteen years berating,
thrashed in the fissure of love,
never soothed, impossible to know how comforted you
might have been, murdered in your daughter's eyes,
a vendetta without compunction,
like you, ambivilantly despised,
despising in turn,
making certain no one comforts with the touch,
leaving us our imagined ideals
in shades of drying blood.

6

A fantasist's world rendered in shades of black,
sour urine, crippled knees, organs of complicity,
eternity to eternity fetched & retrieved,
this family broken of itself against itself,
leaving its survivor to record cruelty & sadness,
having become our eternal dialogue.

7

Father,
we noticed your impromptu self-portrait on the note
telling us you went for coffee to salve the glands,
to pump the adrenals for another day.
The drawing touches some obscure reference,
a moustache I didn't detect until your daughter clearly
pointed out the telltale feature,
what looked like the downward slope of a coverlet
to the back of the head, with no eyes or mouth,
a moustache in pen
flaring forth sadly humorously along
the rendering's outer edge taking us beyond the leaves.

8

Father,
there are twelve more hours to ponder uncertainty,
visible and conjured scenes you spend
conjuring fear more fear threats fears
more fears of death & loss,
so irrational you have no idea
the well-placed rationale I lay before you,
insisting on the sick flavor of your satiated nightmares,
rats in the yard, mice in the basement,
persecution if you resist,
fearing the unconscious, the murk of insanity,
weakness of flesh, holding leviathans in the dark,
some terrifying vision of demise,
fear and fear and fears multiplying shapes in the night,
tying the dog to your side,
a bloody heart dropped at your feet

9

Leaves barely move in their wake below summer sun,
no sound buried under wheel in the driveway,
or chirping birds, closing doors as if to slip away
mysteriously in some rite
to engage some private conversation on porch or patio.
Sometimes even as I approach,
the air round with impenetrable inviolability,
like thickets purposefully planted around the house,
their words keep wind from blowing away,
their heavy earth,
their heads in absentia as they move off each morning,
wondering who tastes first the bitter acrimony of death.

10

Sister, you took back the letter you left on my desk
because you were embarrassed,
because our self-imposed exile as brother & sister
at such distance in our minds
weighs down the unknown,
those swollen parathyroids now removed
buying temporary reprieve from the end.
You must keep talking, even at night,
because that fear of utter void touching your walk
is one brave glimpse into the future
there is no way to know.

11

Since mother has become expert at the grand illusion,
all roads lead back to first cause
not pretending to the beautiful,
not couched in flowery terms,
but Roman realities, warts & scowls, pock-marked faces
& inner pestilence,
all logic, not poetry, but meant to be what it is,
even if holding the mirror reflects insipid stupidities,
no matter how close the blood strangled on consensus
below the surface of death.
How can it be beautiful in yearning
when there's hardly poetry left?

12

I watch you in silence, sister,
turning my face away because I have no more words,
not certain you want me to find them.
You touch your finger to the arm
that gets the spot of gland & no one knows how long
it must go on, even the bitterness.
walking that final step,
but there comforts the return to appease the last suffering
if it's decided quickly,
the suffering not worthy of life's decline
all in one swoop.

13

This year mother watches two broods of sparrows
under the porch's eave,
babies she doesn't want to see die.
Even she admits the cycle pulsing though their eyes
arrives soon enough.
She reaches with branch beneath tree,
angled back to the leaves, sorrowfully reflecting
their weakness to fly, but flying nonetheless,
three nests of sparrows having brood their liquid,
lamenting their awkward circles of first flight,
burying their dead in solemn repose,
her knees stiffened in arthritic time.

14

Sister, your disease is a barrier harboring molecules
that sieve the denial you've recreated
eighteen years later,
at first the disease, now the fate,
both inextricable connections you fail to see.
But the brutality of words,
that crippling tumor beginning in the mouth,
that feeling bloodless & dehydrated,
ironically keeps you alive.
Disease apparently absolves conscience,
the war you fight firmly established in fatal choices
you don't see having assumed a life its own.

15

There is no way to explain the crushing weight
wrecking the molecules of time with one sweep
in your eyes,
beating at the peripheries of your heart,
the bottomless tears washing father's face,
you upstairs, face averted even at night,
where no one can see, but we who love you,
wringing numbness each day from our solitude even now
nearer clouds that billow in humid light above our heads.
I see you each morning asleep in the arms
of the London lounge as if a tired doll,
wanting to touch your hand, each memory alive & poised,
so stoic under the circumstances,
a front to pretend the sky always looks so light
compared to my words,
little realizing your struggle has made us bitter
to the revelation of existence in knowledge of your fight.

16

Seventy years
slide from languid lines worn to the bone,
tortured bronchial vessels strained to fatigue.
Listen, father, walk carefully because it's so treacherous,
that spirit of decay circling your crushed will
on slopes so gentle the grass bends
before you have time to wake.

17

The Pythagorean number has stopped breathing,
only the morning silent sleeping
with memories over her throat measured by inches,
coagulated blood along the cut,
incision to incision, straddled to her steps,
our father in rapid prayer vigilizing the hour
when light hardly touches time,
the suspension of our lives balanced
on thirty capsules every three hours,
till 7 days later she exits the overworld,
taking her place again under a maddening tinnital roar
reminding us we carry her time without conscience,
paced like beasts of burden,
having stood by her numbers,
deferring our last touch to the hour.

18

I realize
the frozen moment thaws to some purer moment
wherein thinking becomes the tourniquet of reality
etched inside a flowering word that springs to attention
like morning air at 7AM,
the obscure protest of a dog,
this wakened hour that, like me, finds rivers that forget
the orphic tool shaped inside the heart.

19

Father,
I struggle with you
when you want to press a notion home,
when I feel persistence in your effort.
Your wisdom broadens into currents I don't see,
but your infinitesimal voice,
the love you find difficult to express,
your despondency so near I reach to comfort
the beginning & end in some half-shaped reality
sorted out with prayer,
keeping your soul from crushing itself,
adding up to an *espiritus santos*
no other perpetuities hold in the space of this life.

20

Sister,
I see betrayal behind your gestures,
open smiles that die.
My heart drops silent, an air of disbelief
crushed by the weight of foresight,
stopped cold at the door that leaves me naked & alone,
not for my sin, but yours,
too sensitive in the face of pain & decline,
the flower of other leaves whispering,
the numb silence of my slinking form,
forty-one years of compassion shaping my mouth,
your violence tearing away any last shred of faith
in years that have turned the hammer.

21

I feel with my heart
this sick odor of decline,
burdened & liberated by knowledge of failure & sickness,
you don't realize, or if you do,
removed & uncomforted by the sacrifice of body & egos.
There is a brief disease before flight, promises & torment
like phantoms appear, so difficult, I pass saying nothing,
believing no longer the root that has no substance,
betrayed by insecurity & doubt,
the fear that takes them to that shore of trouble
knowing no belief.

22

Father,
you sit watching the dispossession of your soul
you can't forestall, except through fragrant tears
painted against the bay window,
a raised hand hello good-bye when I return,
a shade of a smile cracking worn lips of depression
in the blood of my steps, a shadow of shadows.

III

1

Isn't it fate, father?
I'm telling you it's simple,
the thing most dreaded, if not appeased, the unexpected,
the same eternal question justified & rejustified.
Maybe fear is the greatest catalyst
in your sphere of self-denial,
too blind or frightened to resolve.

2

Empty coats
they are each strangers to words,
three in a line, hung in dry winds.
Here my hands touch the soul of this sleeve & that,
mother father sister,
here my disillusionment escaping along
somnolent shoulders deathlike in stillness…
here words I couldn't speak, begging in silence,
anguish to the end…my eyes running the full length
of memories & colors, shapes & gaits in darkness,
this family of presence without presence.
Perhaps they too will wake at my touch,
empty in essence, the endless whistle of winds
whirling in decline.

3

Their figures move from room to room,
waiting for the unknown,
a pang of hunger, a broken tendon,
endless sleep, irrational hours of insomnia
waiting for non-arrival, ennui assuredly,
shuffling through painful parodies of existence,
death painted across their darkened mouths,
their positions unchanged in hopeless, seedy fatigue.

4

Our father complains,
biting sapphires of time somehow working
the edge of death…
at this distance over the light you're listening, brother,
but do you hear his cold torment, if only less harsh,
this morning two days after Christmas?
It must be freezing in his blood
who art vocal at the door & silenced,
who can't live without shivering.

5

In terrible syntax
their eternal cry burns me to the shallows of my neck,
in vagrant images the hollow of my hand crying
their thrashing murmur, their winter memorizing
my distance revealed to the bone,
at the brink of their trials
no one forced, but circumstance,
no one found, but my years,
no one grieved my rage at their ignorance,
no one forgiven at the door,
no more, mother, no more, father,
no more, sister, no more, brother, no more laughing
humility to comfort the fictions I write.

6

The picture isn't pretty, mother,
we in our grey pallored world of bay windows spying the
ephemeral eye, the woods running to vague distances,
winter's morbid droppings,
white sheets hanging over the sink, a grey pallor over your
hands gingerly scrubbing endless stains of feces
rolling between cracks of wobbling thighs & buttocks,
more like death-shrouds soaked in the ephemera of sleep,
terror, dreams & decay begging to be washed,
but impossible to remove…
the buttons have decayed, keeping the loose threads of
decline from bleeding a cold reality straight to the eyes.
Mother, if all this labor is the shroud,
then where do we fit in our vigil…
if all–as you say–is impossible to alter,
then what is this corrupt notion of love I harbor?
The sheets are so heavy hanging in shallow reservoirs we
build that if you let me take them out of hand,
I'll carry the end that wraps around the desperation in our
eyes, lost in our final belief that something carries on.

7

There is no god in their universe inflicting pain,
like sparrows hunted on spears,
buried under the weight of their twisted, tormented souls
wounded to the point of pleasure.
My silence is that great reservoir of preservation
they cannot touch except in decline
like sweet flowers created on other waves & winds,
poems like epiphanies of resolve in my heart,
recording their paths of small memory,
gods of self-loathing, therein no more faith,
having ruined each other in ignorance & delight.

8

I resist applying reason to their insanities,
have let go the decay of their lives to retain memories
no more reaching clear thought or sated heart,
never existing except in absentia
as elusive as the new thought that marches
effortlessly to the marginal death,
even further faded recollections of their lives.
Strange this feeling of absent discourse,
time's moveable frame adjusted to some inner mirror
they've lost as if dispersed by deeper light.

9

Mother,
the day after Good Friday
when the resurrection of your tears is most intense,
the sun slips away early.
They aren't invisible, your tragedies,
unrecorded, but not unspied.
I turn my back momentarily, a third-person entity
that drifts passed your tears,
but you don't see, or if you do, pretend I don't observe
your diffuse flow of grief & self-pity
over a shattered psyche, wordless motherhood,
disillusionments that shape each carotid artery
into gargantuan crimes sprung from the clock
I wind one hour forward ticking above us.

10

Father's pissing can't wait because it's all falling
to some indistinguishable point of no return,
when the artificial dark that shapes his countenance
becomes the face that has no more features,
his crushed soul falling from the rafters,
aggrieved of his final days.

11

Since the shell is all that's left,
the endless debate that goes on room to room
like Sisyphean labor concludes nothing,
the purpose of such dialogue to placate the molecules
without disturbing the sense,
since sense tells us, sister, your conversation is pointless.
We're listening to you ramble, but placated time
marches steadfast over the earth you call home,
having missed the meaning of existence,
struggling to pyrrhic victories over a beaten family,
emptied, denuded by your words.
We can hardly listen anymore to your trial
of afflicted milk poured from the womb.
Look, words can walk like burdened figures touching
the earth, but your cruelty leaves only the soulless heart
affixed to that thread of vein keeping us alive
to your torment.

12

Having turned against father in hatred,
mother & daughter destroy him,
the man-hatred of mother in daughter,
yet thinking himself innocent,
he too pays the price of denial,
vengeance finding him the perfect sacrifice.

13

This tangled web of sexual spleen
spit from the mouths of the lost...
it's a knife to the heart,
an inverted snake emerging from the orifice
of familial betrayal & hatred always denied.

14

To my surprise father & daughter are measuring a truce
at the incongruous hour of 8:13 am,
rubbing souls like cats after battle,
sharing their communal lives arched over television,
showing the retired stirring popcorn in cauldrons
on the streets of Kansas City,
the tender measurement of their lives captured at last
as if the weather theirs,
their trails like archealogic patterns leading eternally
to bed & kitchen, sofa to bed,
perhaps to yard, a short car ride.
They don't know the sun is balancing outside
their bay window in bright shafts still & frozen,
a white shade to keep out & no space between
making their way back to bed in shaped shadows, passive
inhabitants waiting on the unknown,
servants to the next step they've already memorized,
but for one that records, like a movie, their mesmeric lives
each minute, each second out of 13 in 8, their precarious
lips of asyphixation in each breath they think is theirs
forever.

15

Standing by my right shoulder, sister,
you are as far from me as the fractured axis,
at once loving, then hating, but hating more
the existence that dies in each breath turning to the wind,
pouring over pets a lost love for humans,
walking the tense steps of death,
forgetting the source of love, only the sadistic stream.
It isn't your life anymore.
The *oeuvre* of true self can't be trusted,
because we only love that which no longer exists,
the parrot of talking eruptions,
my eyes turned away from the tourniquet
of your false hope.

16

White blossoms falling this spring mark a trail that follows
your precipitant time
between those blossoms like snow fluttering to earth,
at first in confusion, but once there
laying a distinct path you don't recognize.
I ask where you're going.
You laugh under your breath an ironic, painful emptiness
you recognize, for you have nothing,
standing on these fleshy white blossoms
as if one with the dead in a pallor of sunlight,
cast in sickly yellow over your troubled face,
turned among the branches,
touching your life in their shade.

17

Mother, you nearly took that eternal flight
borne ahead star-shaped with hieroglyphic fingers at the
crown of your head that moved like a comet into the tail
of the unknown, your equanimity a marvel of timing
beyond fatalism, sitting at the kitchen table,
assuring me the bruise directly above your hairline
is only a micro-cosmic ordeal of pain,
even though you thought father should have stopped
the flight of the unexpected taking you & he
from the known to the unknown in seconds
too swift to replay the spreading web of fracture
you created just short of night,
pouring its dull effulgence into your mouth,
open at a shout, then shut on horror of impact,
your head spinning into new creation,
death just short of speaking the peace you thought
traveled from one point to another,
stunned at the ineptitude of fate, calmly assessed out of
fists of placation.

18

Like you, sister, there is no other option but to offer
sustenance over the barrier...there the dog's snout,
the sound of grass pressing under it paws,
you too having perception,
having brought you to this place
partially above, peering into lassitudes,
measuring the hopeless step, the optimistic moment,
the shattered revelation there crawling on earth
in tormented appeals to freedom.
The night draws you to the fence,
a frantic dog smiling its pleasure
painted in humid twilight on the brink of inevitabilities.

19

Your shadows cast other shadows I cannot separate
from the cloak of grey you insist on painting,
but isn't it only the formality of depression
shaped around your sanctified psychoses?
All your steps follow a path of misery over my heart,
three shadows stretching the bonds of familial love
I no longer recognize in this fractured sanctuary,
listening to your plaintive calls,
a wheezing door, a vigil of demise you call living,
willing my death into your hands.

20

The flower outside the rear door has a beauty
that belies happiness,
that mine is non-existent, even to your eyes,
even to your touch as strangers
reduced down to the bone in time's acidic bath,
the touchstone of my senses,
the wonder you still exist, but as ghosts cloaked
in patterns of mixed grey,
now covering us the color of dust,
the nothingness I face in your sickness.

21

I note your expression frozen in humid light, too, sister.
an arm leaning on the fence, the particular angle
of your feelings expressed over a mouth
of poison & disdain,
like cancer intruding without knowledge,
transforming you into personified evil.
First one thought, then another, somehow contrary,
you are fixed in one pose of boiling decline
no one can fix.

Those cavernous shades of atrophied emotion
play in contrast to the innocent leaves above you,
rising & falling in slow, endless decline.
Your worst fear is the one already realized,
but the mercy is you're not aware the shattered axis
forces you to calibrate your eyes to their cyclic season
endlessly counted for the ones inflicted,
forever in that shadow of existence stripped of reason,
wandering lost in nightmare,
memorized in this fragmentary picture of futility
etched forever in my eyes.

22

The brutal asphyxiation of their lives burns in sunlight,
the dyspepsia of emptiness filling despair,
the sun frozen in fixity, working them like dough
into the refuse of dormancy, anchored in spirited acids
like rivers of drained hours,
lived by persistent gnawing of death,
spying the sun like ravenous animals,
watching the lost mile of their anguish.

IV

1

We residing together
are now sleeping below the fifth parallel of a world
rising over the eaves, wet with words frozen to the silence
of this house leaning into decay.
The fence encircles a fragrant shadow
embedded in still foliage,
flowers sprinkled liberally around the perimeters of our
last dwelling, purple flowers permeated with bees,
the nectar of my heart-bleed,
images & sounds begging separation, racing for reprieve,
the harsh scrapping of a chair pushed from the table,
mother's plaintive cry haunted by pursuit,
the catafalque of my thoughts etched in pallid miracles
living on the edge of sunlight.

2

I stand back turned to exuding earth,
cool in the steam of worms & wolves,
walking ineluctable paths to sorrow & survival.
For one moment the membrane of late morning waits
like some blue line of affirmation
I am privileged to indulge,
the sun in brazen coat of arms weakly retreating to
a hanging leaf, a severed pair of branches,
a scourge of timeless hours marching in repose.

3

My dreams are sapphires burning a flagellant past
no longer calm,
the experiential prison of one over two,
two over three, three concluded on four,
a rhetorical question always bounding forth from
the salivating jaws of imprisonment,
the center disintegrating before my eyes
no longer able to tell the difference
between laughter & crying, dying & sleeping,
resistance or death.

4

I am watching & listening to the tears of my steps,
years of assonance attached to what was…
in the shadow of infinite prepositions,
in prose poems of afternoons
tormenting me with promise,
in a flower's septic sweetness trying to revive my senses,
helping this tired step that momentarily falters & lifts
to optimism again.

5

The poem of this silence is the death of my hours,
formed around clouds that pour their
effulgence into disillusionment,
the key that no longer fits the door,
lifted momentarily by time's glandular motion,
as clouds barely shade the sky in momentary bliss.

6

Mother,
sometimes there is one instrument of hatred,
if released prevents you from containing it,
destroying the one sanctuary you've known
on these bitter, familial slopes, reprehensible & pitiless,
your daughter the tool through which you revenge
yourself, hers but the satisfaction of crushing
out the father standing in her way...
you, mother, allowing vengeance to bloom,
failing to decry her work,
allowing the betrayal you deservedly suffer,
she having her cross, but you carrying the nails.

7

Father,
there are images that freeze the cornea,
one etched in black last night,
your figure in bold dimensions taking me by surprise,
standing legs apart, hands in pockets,
shroud in blackness, no detail of your face visible,
observing me return from my own somnolent journey.
Father, you were greeting me without words,
taking me by surprise…it bears repeating,
because it confused my perception of you,
an illusion of regained stature,
an illusion of what you once were.
Forgive my heartbreak…the eye deceives,
living along these obscure lines of shadow joining us
forever poised by eternal cries refusing to pacify the night.

8

Sister, the wind shades your tragic step,
your shadow in the window, one hand raised,
the other calling back the light bouncing off my palm…
do you know the day reduces your fractured reality
into my hands, the tension of your life like a blade cutting
through the viscera?

9

I reach down into the black pool you offer up before me,
as if some Etruscan mirror
telling me we are dressing the catafalque,
my eyes fixed on its shiny surface
above flowers still blooming in October.
This isn't paint you offer with two hands,
but death in masquerade, bled from the source.

10

I can still read your thoughts with back turned,
but you still don't make that forward step
that must lead somewhere...
instead your repetitive absolutions flow into one
continuous stream of insomnia
after the final drop of water has settled in your palms,
a miracle you're still not cognizant,
pondering that last course making you fear the unknown,
burdening you with doubts you can't forebear.
I too wash under the same absolutions,
for we have made this ourselves like bread denuded of
wonderment, hours hoarded of dreams,
memories pinned to dangerous fictions long passed,
an alarm going on & on,
but no hand to stop it.

11

I live in dampness bathing my chest,
groping fortresses not mine,
inheriting this edifice lacerated on the jaws of death.
I taste bitter, transparent dust that washes away the leaves,
crumbled in red heaps in the circle of my arms,
the shoulders of clouds no longer lilting on the horizon,
an endless stream running through my heart
between beats, the rush of vein & artery
finding other paths to solitude.
I concentrate on one aperture,
one clear spear balancing my heart,
a flower of dust bent to the ring of other powers,
capturing this relentless tower of autumnal rain,
crying its mournful clatter, running its pluralistic vine.

12

Stretched on your back like some humbled christ,
this placating, you understand,
is only a part of compassion always disabused,
but you have only one step memorized, father,
having forgotten the magic that transforms you into me
in that disabused universe of misery you walk
in dragging steps to the infinite decay.
I press the eye of the calf where your pain sings
its vile news between my fingers,
lifting your mottled foot to the light,
recognizing its strained Da Vincian angles,
offering you instead the temporary shelter of my hands,
pressing your nerve-throb in concert with fate,
framed in the lost hope I try to bring with a son's love.

13

In a rain of sun showering shadows across earth,
my steps proceed in effortless wind along its edge,
the purity of its presence framing this space
around my soul dusting faded stars,
metaphors retrieved, one foot beyond the other,
the *enfant-exuberant* remembering their eternal presence.

14

I stand inside an October sun
taking in the blue as water moves eternally away
like a million-waved school of fish into channels beyond,
listening as this brief interlude of reality
is filtered clean of its miniscule idea of self,
piercing my heart in tragic rapture.
And I wonder the broken seeds at my feet perusing earth
on the periphery of wind, behind the death of my fathers
& forgotten music fused to the ceiling of time
the weak grass reaches slowly
the dying touch where I think of this passage of bridges,
stark-dead fields left to the mouths of horses
languidly at their pace,
husked by the silence of placid hours.

15

Here then father are the final fragments you ask I bring,
the scattered ephemera of newsprint,
the odorless decay of despondency,
the snow-pasted windows of midday,
the eternally pounding hand of death
crying for more sleep,
the cracked notions of the world,
the insipid idea of irrationality you exemplify,
the explanations you refuse to digest,
the blindness to words I speak,
the fragrant memory of yesterday,
the bitterness of reality,
the cold infusion of my presence asking for reprieve,
the dying whisper of a day,
the fractured signs of love burning the lost fire in my eyes.

16

My poems have died,
fragments made to walk miles more when all is lost,
backs broken, reducing all to a single point
in the palm's shadow where light plays underneath the
skin, forcing veins to surface.

17

I once imagined the reality of my life
greeting the day in happy whispers–
but now I fracture its imagery before it arrives,
unburdening the terminality of my backbone
broken into pieces of trembling fuel,
burning the externality of existence.

18

A blue harbor cuts into my eye like a strip of ocean,
sunlight glittering on its shield.
Time rolls beneath us tracing a muddy path
across a city landscape,
its latitude sketching
the unknown terror of the self...
how the motor runs facing the insurmountable
how the rain pummels
how the flesh exploits
how the heart bends proliferates lies & congeals
when eyes betray the mouth betraying the word
betraying the thought betraying the soul
to some form of liberation
the world masquerades.

19

My silence is that great reservoir of preservation
they cannot touch except in decline
like sweet flowers created on other waves & winds,
poems like epiphanies of resolve in my heart,
recording their paths of small memory,
gods of self-loathing, therein no more faith,
having ruined each other in ignorance & delight,
buried under the weight of wounded souls.

v

1

Here in this heartbroken world without compromise,
in the shadow of my repetitions,
in the vague sleep of inspired dreaming,
the particulars of existence...
here in my palm
the pained realizations,
the offal of economic deliberations,
breaking along a descending poetic line that traces
a path of shattered arteries,
a crippled idealism,
a voice of irreconciliations.

2

There is no poetry I can touch here.
I struggle to maintain the day's dying whisper,
the eternal riding & unease,
the night wet, quiet & calm lights glowing,
paths darkened street to street,
the blinking eye closed, this corner of the universe,
guitar staring in utter silence,
permeating my heart.

3

My mother's apology, my sister's good-bye,
my father's darkness,
the Christmas tree late, but there nonetheless,
bathed in red…two poems at once,
night & family & immanent decay borne on the hour.

4

As long as we have known silence, father,
as shadow is light & light shadow,
as we know grief in words & deny them,
burdened by practical concerns, nothing more,
as we know this reality,
this unforgivable silence & restraint,
as long as death hides behind voices,
like unending shadows no longer recognized
so I hear your words dying as we have time left to live,
murdered in your blindness
that put to death the son in me.

5

I once refused to express life's bitterness,
thinking it betrayal of ideals,
refusing to acknowledge my soul's reduction to ashes,
spitting out bones.
I wanted to crack the bull's back & grab the horns
aching against my lips.
Life slips & dies in my grasp,
the heart burns its bridges,
trees cornered on pinnacles waiting for spring…
in my blood the trials of slow pace,
a dialectic polishing its knives before my eyes
& the fatigue of nests,
the cry of arriving birds to their roosts…
there is too much silence in this to bear memory,
waiting for the sun to reinvent its edifice of power.

6

This morning is a broken minute
standing languid before me,
still I watch myself evolve into a liquid entity,
devoid of substance a substance my own,
a poetry of dead religion dripping from dead hands.

Words are somber in the morning,
words of resolution, words of dead youth, flesh & bone,
dying in the very heart of things,
weighing me against every murdered ideal,
a rush of wind glazing the tongue,
crows surveying the landscape from their highest perch
beside winds higher up…calmly, frighteningly cold.

7

There are times I fall into rhetoric.
A verbalism of failed promise.
An xyz indulging its irreality.
A river below us still blessed.
A sky's fever drenched in the sun's barren shadow,
an avian cry brooding another season.

8

I read Machado this morning & blessed the potted plants,
my mother's seeds, leaves on the ground,
silent sunlight, northern winds, open spaces
& dogged steps, simple language & historical tracts,
libraries & stately branches,
quiet streets, reflections of light & shadows that creep
along the curb around the heart,
squeezing the last ounce of memory from my words.

9

I remember the backwater of my youth,
steps that led nowhere,
eyes that saw nothing,
dreams that paled in sunlight,
hopes that shriveled with disillusionment…
pallid steps staring up at a haunted gaze,
art talk that rebounded nowhere, friends lying through
their teeth inside a dead world, walking, talking,
shaping dead words with their mouths.

10

Isolation is an open window impossible to close,
soothing & distraught,
making its way inside the skull…
a broken tool of logic,
a twisted piece of protoplasmic weaponry,
an eye a nose an ear, a demiurge of existence,
an image a frame a dead world struggling to revive.

11

The poetic irreality of a headache…
but it's been so many times before that the perspective
sans the headache appeals to me more…
clear eyesight, unjaundiced viewpoints,
free thoughts free being free existence pursuing
an endless dialogue of life & death…
that everything is merely a description of life rather than
life itself…people who cannot have,
people who cannot act, people who cannot feel,
reveling in their own peculiar form of death.

12

Where does it ring against the blue that slips
on the coolness of earth, on wind, through the blinds
that order in their numbers another world,
segmented & bright?
We have watched it each season,
and watch it each day, the otherness of the world
outside beyond the blinds playing back & forth
against the air, the light, that with the leaves
rubbing our bay window that blows straight furiously,
the calm behind the glass,
that I watch this scene repeat itself,
or tricks to the eye,
that I see something other crossing the parallel lines
of blinds that lazily blink & hesitate,
that my vision is all that matters
that reality has not changed but for me,
that it is all really perception & nothing more,
that the indomitable world is indomitable to the end,
its changes so subtle so steady so secret we fail to see.
This scene is art at least in its primal sense,
for as I observe the leaves fall back & forth between the
lines, I am reminded of this other world separate from
me, but right at hand.

13

I stroke fifty years by a hair,
a breathe, a prayer to leaves in repose,
no anger or anguish, biology having its way,
the heart once so obscure, so real, moving destinies…
the sun I see, the wind that fails,
the metaphysical speech no longer resonating…

The knowledge others create,
swallowing their cynicism I renounce,
written out of negation, not reason or passion,
negation of family, negation of world, negation of words,
negation of light, negation of history, negation of self,
negation of limits, negation of time…

14

Trees sketched in shadows
that don't move unless wind commands,
that don't breathe unless earth moves,
shimmering stillness & thinness of mist & cloud
blanketing their surface…
an image of sunlight melting in summer.

15

I promised myself no postscript, no last words,
no additions or subtractions,
but leaves aching above us
and your staggered walk without feeling...
and you're walking toward me, father,
as if eager for words, dying in my eyes,
a weakened spirit, battered & shrapneled.

16

I think of my lost world,
silent walls that comforted my grief,
sanguine meditations no threat to the world nor myself.
I think of that world I can no longer reach,
bathed in night air, a different logic, deaths in shallows,
a scrapping irregularity of heartbeat...
walking freely no more, struggling with the grinding
silence of irresolution & grief...and happiness,
a word of tranquil substance, a metaphor for dissipation.

17

Leaves contain a secret shade
& winds that mysteriously breathe
weigh the measurements of earth, the liquid eye pressing
into the essential cavities of existence.

What then of the sweet exteriorization of life–
is it ever anything but the moment grinding into my side?
Maybe it's there beneath the stove
or singing in the glasses.
The wine is cold, but my lips are singed on words,
uttered too deep & resonant like a cloud.

18

Father,
I repeat myself in duplicated expressions
that try those barriers, still hoping to breach
this bad light making you look sicker
than you are in that noiseless nothingness
of existence that overwhelms conscience
with inconsequentials,
your shoulder blades like bony leviathans
falling to the deep.
I resolve to stay my distance,
preserving our words fallen soundless between us,
more rejected than embraced,
content with their superficial engagement,
still thinking something will affix us as father and son,
a message, a last coda, a dropping of the guard.

19

And the sun with its leaning head of cloud,
the darkened roads,
searching for the passage that buries its fuel,
peering from the dark of its sanctuary ...

And the soft grey earth sinking beneath my feet
as we walk on, our feet caught in ruts
leading to the sun ...

And the sun along avenues,
framed & purified ...

20

It took me an hour, she said.
Sweating, pulling, shaping, discarding a patch of grass.
The only place that receives sun all day, she points out.
A smudge of dirt on her upper forehead.
My mother's troubled forehead weighed down by the sun.
Let's go in the shade, she said relievedly.

On the green grass,
on the soft, effluent earth, as if barefoot again,
I wake to her grief without notice.
Look at the flowers, she said, telling me again & again
last year's never seeded & died.

21

The blinds create a prismatic effect
of leaves blowing in the wind.
Sometimes I'm transfixed.
Looking at an unexpectedly revealed reality
of the external world, the eye's perception is altered
without work, without plan,
unexpectedly exteriorized by force of image,
leaves swaying, bending in the wind.

22

I measure my father's view from the bay window.
I determine precisely the angle of his vision.
The living room in shadows.
His words eager to come,
but silence leaving us speechless.

Father, I must leave.
His eyes fleck with fatigue & emptiness,
that eternal fear of loneliness in his eyes.

23

A sound deepens even the sky.
A wind, a scattering of clouds, the frantic squabbles of
sparrows, picking the trees of bruises, their slight, cool
shadows rustling summer's first hot breezes,
a sanctuary I cannot reach but in imagination.
A tired pace of forty-five years, prayed over,
transitioned & light – now only moments of ennui,
the great leveler, having broken through
these arbitrary gates of conscience.

I wonder what my poetic substance is now–
is it the self in all its redundancy,
the tired images of nature's cyclical mirage,
history & its artifacts, or something alien,
something unseen breathing similes & metaphors,
sucking the marrow from my veins in some
hieroglyphic whirlwind of improbable need?

No one knows I've reached the fatal turn,
the decisive moment, the feared encounter
with nothingness, having nothing more than language,
counteracting the poison of self-delusion.

24

The shadow of youth passes quickly,
so it cannot be the thing of ultimate worship,
the flesh-vibrancy of wondering,
the blinding spell of love & the mercurial nature
of change–nor can it be deification of old age,
senilities & freezing limbs,
cynical words & checkers in summer.

It is somewhere between
avenues of aspiration and idealism, self-realization
& desire to become the implicit self,
having no competition but the worst elements of the self
and the most praiseworthy, between moral lapses
and ethical superiorities, between dying words
& the reborn syntax.

25

In the painfully brilliant corner of idealism.
In the mortified time of my aging step.
In the liberation of this poetic line outside the rangling of
misconstrued literary theories, eternal steps lead nowhere,
neither here nor there,
neither realist nor spiritualist,
this heart softens to each & in each imprints the soul.

Once the wind clears the path before me,
then & only then,
when our spirit bonds to a happy miracle,
so our eyes search the cold & expectant.

26

O father of mortified expectations.
O mother's burning limbs with shame.
O sister's bleeding metaphors,
pains that have us groveling in disaffection.
O language beyond comfort & expurgation.

Was there ever misery like this?
Everything loved, reflecting a super-attenuated reversal?
Everything touched as if extending to the fingertips
and no further?
Everything earned by trial & error, faith & determination?
Everything known, meaning & consequence?
We who sanitize the libido, glorify the aberrant & forever
speculate on the inauthentic, while leaves cry in their
undoing.

27

There is no more misery to fear,
for the sun blazes shadows in reds that burn away
mourning.

The memories of distant cities ruminate in darkness,
having become mired in transformed realities that chase
us into middle-age.

How have we been living?
How have we been dying?

28

I once believed in the world's leviathan circle,
its moonlight, seascapes, torrents & flavors.

But the wind shadows us, the noun soars over us,
the night caresses our gravitations.

The smell of apricots drifts into the air.
A breeze blows through the humid night before us,
voices rising in laughter, diminishing after midnight.

29

We who know the world die in acquisition of the soul,
the shallow miracle we pledge…

we who feel the mirror's silence we cannot face
as flowers drown & die…

we among us who feel the brilliance of a laughing heart
rise in our golden hour between each memory
that records the minute we arrive below
this sky that feels no mercy.

30

Now the transformation is complete.
The rendering of what was into what never can be again,
the years of progress, the slim gait,
the easy, arrogant lassitude,
assumed all the time in the world.

Now they must look twice
to detect once obvious features
buried under shockingly lagged flesh,
unrecognizable even to our deepest selves in the mirror,
avoiding every opportunity to glance at our pathetic
decline into middle-age, while every technology preserves
the severed images of our past.

31

The inevitable witness
presses into us with an indifference that belies the truth,
without the vaguest semblance on the tongue,
impossible to speak words suckled at 86°.

Each terrible terminality of sun is dust in our mouths,
framed in silence, engaging eternal talks
of miniscule dramas we are forced to play out in private.

My tears are shaded angles difficult to see,
points of hazy light in my mother's face,
turned in half-profile, glazed, contorted points
of reference in the grayish pallor of my father's falling
metre…and so the promise is broken.

32

The sun spears my heart,
its golden shield blazing across a building's naked facade,
its glorious skin deeply bathed in solid sunlight,
so golden, so unearthly a sky behind, but dying
at the juncture of life & death.

I see too much truth in the sun's warmth,
my heart so distant,
reflected in her bitter skin.

VI

1

We sit waiting for you to come back, sister,
for even the bitchy complaint would be our joy,
immobile in our grief, exchanging memories
as if passing around the last tourniquet
of the hour before your fate
cuts us to the bone…
we stunned like dead flesh laying us naked
in your arms to rest the sweet languor of eternity.

2

I stand under the apple tree
transfixed & amazed at the dying branches.
Mother, you said the tree has been dead for some time
now–"in the middle." I say–"I must cut this branch,"
"I must cut that one," and without hesitation
I find the saw & only manage to cut three small branches
that merely brush my face,
not the blackened, charred limbs that disturb
the notion we can go on living like unwrecked denizens
in our own jungle.

3

Mother,
I did not want you to see
my work or pain, for I sense in your eyes
the haunted belief we can still grow undeterred
like this truth that has saved us its eternal shade…
and then to see one lone apple
among the dying green & grey was too much
the heavy burden of our choice & our dying…
mother, the confusion in your eyes
is sometimes too much to bear,
when the leaves vomit forth their summer green,
yearning for a return to oneness in our sky.

4

O father,
the psalms that cradle the heart
are a heavy burden without your living benediction,
& the love that conceives our shadow
takes us to wordlessness before their light.
I know it now more fervently than ever
in these final words.

There are so many psalms in my heart
you cannot hear now in quiescent tears & frozen breaths
we have earned together–mother, daughter, all adhering
even as we breathe, holding us together,
our only breath the last breath I saw you take
in fractions of a second,
turning head once left, then right & every shadow gone
so quickly turning sallow grey, then cold
& burnished forehead I kissed,
the sheet borne indifferently to your neck
& everyone walking outside the door
& all life & death parading in laughing ridicule.

5

There is no end to the snow
breathing, filling, shaping the morning's falling path.
I study & trace the silent vision limited to the firmament,
my voice learning the endless passage.

We are only calling voices from room to room,
circling our heads in dreams, salvaged by the light.
We talk of soul, we dream of voices,
one step closer to the window stormed by tactile words
that search our eyes for meaning.

6

I want to frame the darkness, mother
extract its magical timepiece piercing my chest there
above the trail of marks leading to my left collarbone
where the pain is too crucial to ignore
when I drive with my left hand & right hand propped
you touch in crying pity & sympathy for my plight
more than your own.

The elm is dying as you foresaw
scratching the eaves stiffly moving dead in its limbs.
I am sad too remembering & pointing & not wanting to
turn around as we talk in painful recollections
& exasperated sighs…and your hands gnarled
with arthritis bending & bulbous at the joints–
still you touch my hand to comfort
our tragic view of reality.

We will wait till spring for the true fate we promise,
we will wait & see whether the leaves come back,
whether we are spilling our blood without purpose.
Let's wait–I agree, mother, it's better to wait until we are
sure of death, until the dog's legs buckle,
until I am forlorn for the last time in your eyes…
mother, we know the tree is like no other, but we insist it
live & maybe it lives to bear tomorrow's weight, the roar
of traffic beneath its tranquil shade.

7

When I see you day by day
descending in subtle steps down the front stairs,
I remember your daughter, you to her left,
her left hand on your right arm, both weak,
but you somehow stronger,
her last walk up the stairs to the house & to the bed.
I carried it down from upstairs & the blood that ended it,
her terrified eyes.

I see all this in those five steps leading to the front door,
that ineluctable truth bearing my eyes to the sunlight
we keep buried, touching your gnarled hand as I drive,
and you say you love me & we cry.
How your steps talk one by one,
convincing me we are resolved standing
in the harshest winds of existence.

8

Father,
I never knew how the body died
in strange warmth, in darkness & light,
leaving me guilty for destroying those oracular ears that
heard & deciphered every tone & musical note,
the cochlear beauty inside your head & hazel-green eyes
that I remember once caught the tiniest print from across
the room, and the hand that chorded guitars
& accordions leaving me in filial wonder at your burnt
ashes in hand.

9

Isolated lights burn & trail off into staid air,
and the self ponders invisible bridges
that keep us moving like indistinguishable islets
of human form no one sees
over this spine of open urban landscape,
turning the soul inside out.

10

Nothing to go back to, nothing that returns,
no forward, no backward,
no one to bake bread, no poems, no light,
no warmth, everything has failed.
Nothing has grown, everything has died,
nothing to save the heart,
coldness without shame, pain without blood,
death without mercy.

11

All who die sweetly
show the dying portion of the day,
every turn of leaf drifting to oblivion.
How close above the shadows
the sun fades, golden & mute, cut from the sky
the rustle of autumn, moving winds
and the shadow of trees, the broken land,
the shade beneath midday,
the sun glancing through leaves like ghosts
floating to earth, my face warmed
to the living source of existence.

12

I memorize the snow promised,
falling in soft whispers from a night sky I barely see.
From where I stand, it is too much night,
too much memory that invades, too much movement,
too many shadows listening to the rustle of my breath
and stifled grief lost on the path of least resistance
& the night I walk to avoid soon beyond my grasp,
measuring out my steps in tortured circles.

13

The body lives on one thin thread
spearing the surface of our thoughts,
invisibly trying our souls to the flesh.

We are left alone on the scales,
weighed against each tear, each laugh in the dark
and touching hands.

The stillness has you shivering in that somnolent world
of no place between earth and sky,
a blue transfixed image of self, aging and quick-eyed,
skimming along the streets,
the lonely trail of eternal steps leading to one more
assault on the conscience.

14

The bushes are cleared at last, mother
letting in the sky that never was,
and if it was lost beyond the highest branches,
they never bent over this earth.
There a gnarled piece of branch left,
twisted & grown inside the fence meshing.
I'll have to take the saw to it
and cut it through, even though it is like
those memories you keep circling whenever
you wash your clothes and take out our family
pictures and point to your children
disappeared among the rushes, even as I point
to the apple tree nearly dead
that surprisingly blooms two or three branches
ahead of the hour, and you're saying not to cut
the dead ones, even the ones that look
charred because you say they are sanctuary
for the birds who have nested forever
under the eaves.

15

We see everything now, mother.
We're the last ones to notice every detail
of what is, what was, what will never be.
You hold up the dried out broken knots
of wood hammered in at the door with
a nail driven through saying, "I can do it."
And that dog barking two yards away
you say must have something wrong with it,
and you say to it under your breath, "That's alright, it's
alright," but I know there's no more comfort in the air
than there is in your awareness that the sky has opened up
to our surprise, and the useless frown of what-for
on the two tomato plants you bought,
pushing them aside on the stove saying,
"That devil weed is back in full-force" as we measure
our dissipation glass by glass.

16

For one second inside the door
you turn and stand still facing the yard,
and I know you are crying,
though I never ask why because I know.
Three times a day, you say, in the morning
when you wake, in the afternoon before sleep,
at night before your final rest.
These prayers, mother, are the endless rosary
that knows no mollifying.
Before I leave you hand me the tomato plant for my yard.
I see in your eyes a tenderness and your tears
disappear momentarily at its life,
its ambiguity dissolving for a moment
after the tears if only to prove how much love
is in you for the living.

17

Those dead branches
are leaning over us now, mother,
scratching the segment of sky between
the porch and the roof.
But then we are used to living with death
and depression day & night,
though I wonder how there can be one charred branch
among the white blossoms.

18

The night has no heart in its stomach,
it wastes away in fragrant shadows
that disappear along the path.
There the steps I see leading to the earth
and the grave step that opens to all assaults of the spirit.
The world's disparities frame this morning
in transparent light, the quiet evil of interpretation
always one moment ahead
when the light freezes against the calm,
when the notion stands still against the backwash
of emptiness inculcating the sky.
It is always the paradoxical notion
of living that marches forward without orders,
without sleep, feverish pathways to the unknown,
there in a barely discernable sign
cracking along the invisible seams of the world.

19

Who knows whether it is light or dark,
the shade alters the shape, but the substance is still light,
still muted in tranquil glory.
Even while it fades & changes,
its angles melting, its purity diffusing and dissipating,
it weakly speaks to solid earth,
sometimes swelling, sometimes fading, but ever-constant
for one poised instant, the inviolable.

20

Has it all come down to us
so broken like a fearful dawn, grey and fractured
at the sky's edge I barely discern?
From where I stand, our very souls look as if they've died,
a facsimile of faces drowned in a fear & hatred
of our own construction.

21

The leaves are arranged in a straight, peaked line
that wait to be swept away by everything mechanical,
everything ordered, everything predicted.
The only consolation is the early morning
when it is possible to sing,
and the cold refreshes as I move back & forth,
separating branches from leaves,
leaves from branches, pausing at their line of demarcation
between earth and sky.

www.ingramcontent.com/pod-product-compliance
Ingram Content Group UK Ltd.
Pitfield, Milton Keynes, MK11 3LW, UK
UKHW041450180426
11946UKWH00013B/140/J